For Alan and Joshua, with love! ~ K.W.

For Jason, Jaden and Jaxon, with love! ~ D.A.

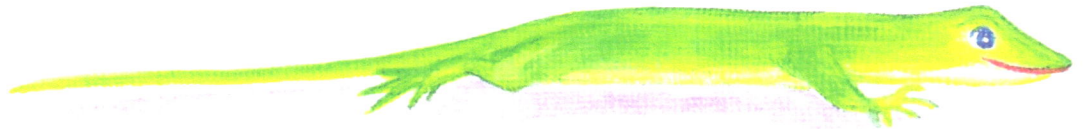

ɯ

Milo Productions, LLC
www.MiloProductionsllc.com

The Lizard and The Dragonfly
Text copyright © 2012 by Kim Whitney
Illustrations copyright © 2012 by Deborah Allison
Printed in the U.S.A. All rights reserved

ISBN 978-0615657233
First Edition

The Lizard
and
The Dragonfly

Written By Kim Whitney

Illustrated By Deborah Allison

It was a warm sunny day in the sand dunes by the sea and the dragonflies were flying around playing their favorite game of tag.

Buzzzz,

Buzzzz,

Buzzzz.

Nearby, there were lizards watching the dragonflies as they swooped and swirled through the air with ease.

One lizard in particular was watching the dragonflies in amazement. His name was Larry.

Larry wished that he could soar through the air like
the dragonflies.

So Larry climbed up on a branch of a tall sea grape tree and jumped off trying to fly.

Larry flapped his arms as fast as he could...

7

but he fell to the soft sandy ground with a thud.

All of his lizard friends laughed and told Larry he was silly to try to fly.

Larry took a deep breath and used a confident voice to say, "I don't like it when you laugh at me. Please stop." Most of the lizards politely stopped but Larry still felt sad.

Larry's lizard friends thought he needed time to himself so they left to go play a game of hide-n-seek in the sea oats.

Larry sat sadly back up on the sea grape branch and watched the majestic dragonflies finish their fun game. He sighed as they flew away.

One dragonfly noticed Larry sitting sad and alone. He decided to stop to ask him what was wrong. This concerned dragonfly was named Daryl.

"My name is Daryl. What's your name?" asked the dragonfly. "Larry," the lizard replied sadly. "Why are you so unhappy?" queried Daryl. "I wanted to fly up in the air," Larry explained, "but my friends laughed at me for trying and then left me to go play among the sea oats."

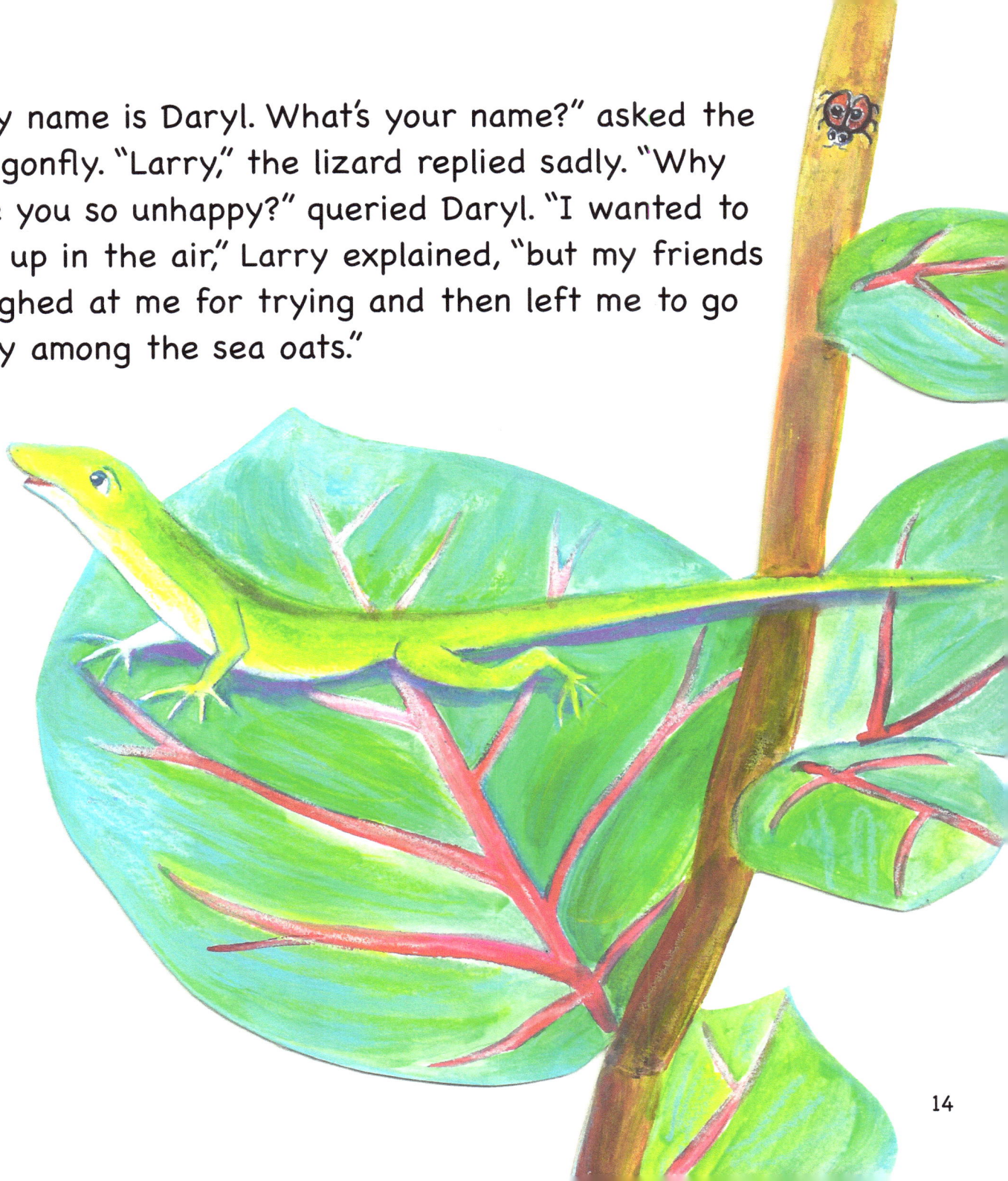

14

Daryl thought for a moment and answered, "When I was younger I wanted to be able to swim under the sea like the mullet fish I saw in the shallow water below me. I almost drowned when I tried to dive under the water. My friends laughed at me too."

"I then realized that I should be happy being a dragonfly." Daryl continued, "I could fly in the air and the fish could not."

16

Daryl asked Larry, "What can you do that is special or different from others?" Larry thought for a minute and then proudly shouted, "I can change colors from green like the leaves to brown like the branches on the trees!"

"Wow, that's wonderful!" Daryl exclaimed, "I can't change colors like that!" This brought a big smile to Larry's face.

Daryl then proclaimed, "I know you cannot fly on your own, but I can help you fly." Larry asked, "How?" Daryl answered, "You can hop on my back and I can give you a ride."

Larry was so overcome with joy that he started celebrating by dancing a happy lizard dance.

With great excitement, Larry jumped on Daryl's back and the pair started flying through the air.

Whoosh, Whoosh, Whoosh.

First, they flew high over the great sand dunes covered in morning glory and sea oats. Next, they flew over the white sandy beach and finally over the sparkling blue ocean water.

As they flew over the ocean, Larry could see a big school of mullet fish swimming along below and it reminded him of the story Daryl told him.

Suddenly, over the horizon, a great big seagull was flying towards Daryl and Larry. Daryl knew the seagull was hungry and that they were in danger.

Daryl landed on the sea grapes that were nearby and whispered, "Larry, turn brown like the branch and hide both of us. Hurry!"

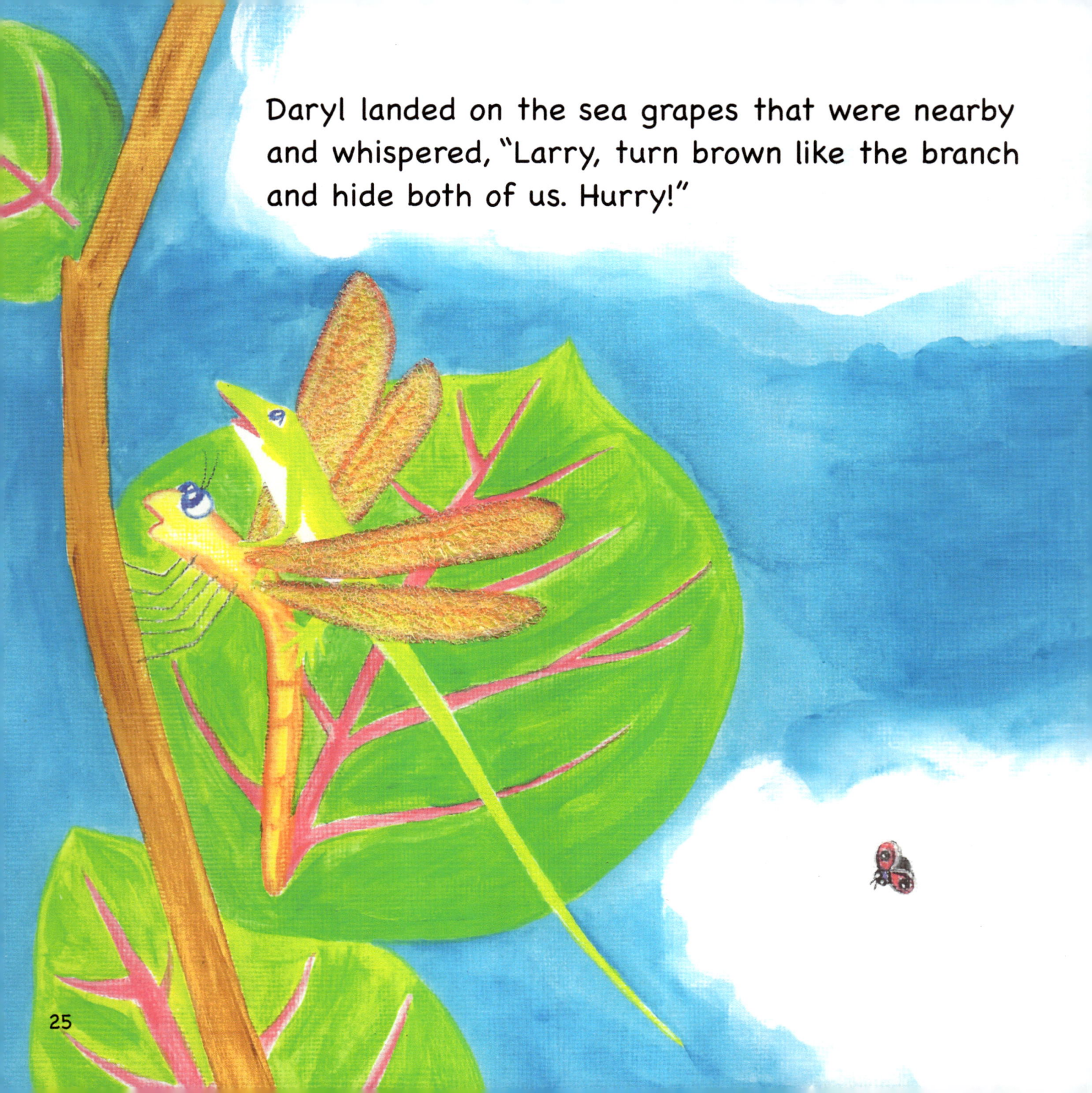

Larry, still on Daryl's back, quickly turned brown and the seagull flew by without seeing them as they were camouflaged and looked like they were part of the tree.

After the seagull flew out of sight, Daryl told Larry, "Because of your special gift to be able to change colors, you saved my life today!"

Larry was grateful he could help his new friend.
He smiled a big proud lizard smile.

As Daryl and Larry flew back over the sand dunes, Larry could see all his lizard friends looking up at him in astonishment.

His lizard friends started to cheer for him as he soared overhead with Daryl.

"Hooray! Hooray!"

After Daryl and Larry landed safely from their adventure, Daryl said goodbye and Larry thanked Daryl for showing him what it was like to fly.

As Larry waited for his lizard friends to run and join him, he thought about what had happened that day. It was then that Larry realized that although it would be great to fly like a dragonfly, he was more than happy to be a lizard that could change colors.

Larry felt happy again.

ACADEMIC APPENDICES

We believe that books are an important part of learning and we are dedicated to helping children learn. As part of this philosophy, we are including appendices that can assist in the educational and social development of children.

The following appendices and information are for the use in academic and social applications of the contents in the preceding story. These can be used in conjunction with the story to help children understand the information in the tale and to apply and augment the educational principles employed in the narrative.

ANOLE LIZARD
\ə-ˈnō-lē ˈli-zərd\

Classification
Kingdom: Animalia (Animals)
Phylum: Chordata (Vertebrate)
Class: Reptilia (Reptiles)
Order: Squamata (Scaled)
Family: Iguanidae (Iguanas)
Genus: Anolis (Anole)

Description: Males are about five to eight inches long. Females are usually smaller and can be less than five inches long. Anoles have adhesive lamellae (plate like structures) on their footpads for crawling along walls. Anoles can change color and can be bright green to brown to gray. Their tails and bodies are long and slender and their heads have pointed snouts. Males have a pink dewlap - a flap of skin that hangs in an arc below their neck. This dewlap is used for attracting females and in territorial displays. Male anoles perform rituals to show their dominance by bobbing their heads, usually through pushup-like movements. They also flare their dewlap.

Habitat: Anoles require greenery, some shade and a moist environment. They can be found in trees, shrubs and on walls or fences.

Food: Anoles eat small insects and spiders. They stalk them in shrubs, vines, walls and even window screens.

Life Cycle: Anoles breed anywhere from late March to early October. Females can lay single eggs every two weeks. These eggs are small, leathery and measure about a quarter of an inch. They need moist soil and foliage and hatch after anywhere from five to seven weeks. They can live up to seven years.

Fun Fact: Male anoles, because of their territoriality, react to a mirror image of themselves and may act aggressively toward it.

DRAGONFLY
\'dra-gən-ˌflī\

Classification
Kingdom: Animalia (Animals)
Phylum: Arthropoda (Arthropods)
Class: Insecta (Insects)
Order: Odonata (Dragonflies and Damselflies)
Suborder: Anisoptera (Dragonfly)

Description: A dragonfly's body length is about one to three and one-half inches. Its two sets of wings are usually held outstretched horizontally at rest. Their back wing is wider than their front wing. The male has three sections to its abdomen (stomach area) while the female has only two sections. Males and females are often colored differently and they have different face color, eye color, color and markings on the thorax (chest area) and wings and different shape, color and markings of the abdomen.

Habitat: Dragonflies live near water and different dragonflies like different water (shaded or sunny, still or moving, fresh or brackish, permanent or seasonal.) Adults can feed at considerable distances from water. Males defend areas of water where females come to lay eggs and females may come to water only for that reason.

Food: Dragonflies eat other insects. Larvae (babies that have not changed into dragonflies) eat other small insects such as mosquito larvae.

Life Cycle: Females lay eggs in or near water; eggs hatch into larvae that remain in water through several molts (shedding of skin) until they are adults. The larvae crawl out of water onto plants and some can crawl many yards from water to find a safe haven. As their skin dries, it splits, and the dragonfly pulls itself out. The young dragonflies are usually pale and unmarked and become colorful over the next several days.

Fun Fact: Larvae breathe through gills in their rectum (hind end); the transfer of water in and out of the rectum is used for moving underwater.

Seagull
\\'sē-gəl\\

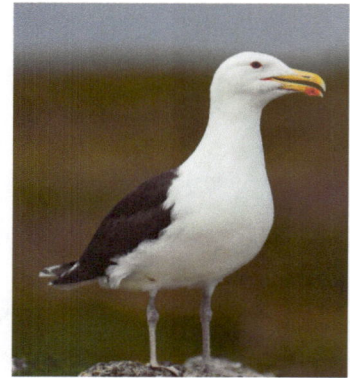

Classification
Kingdom: Animalia (Animals)
Phylum: Arthropoda (Arthropods)
Class: Aves (Birds)
Order: Charadriiform (Medium to Large, live near water)
Family: Laridae (Seagull)

Description: Adult seagulls are about eleven to thirty inches long and are mainly white water birds with a slightly hooked bill (beak), long pointed wings, a short fan-shaped tail and webbed feet. Their head feathers vary seasonally from dirty white/brown to pure white/black and their tail feathers are whitish. Seagull children are often dirty white to brown.

Habitat: Seagulls often nest in colonies mixed in with herring gulls. They nest on a mound of seaweed and other vegetation that is placed on the ground or on a ledge. Their habitat consists of the Great Lakes, coastal beaches, estuaries, lagoons, salt marshes, bays and refuse (garbage) dumps. They are less common on inland lakes and rivers.

Food: The seagull is an efficient predator and feeds on other birds, small mammals, fish, mussels, clams, garbage, rodents and insects.

Life Cycle: The female seagull lays two to four eggs that are olive or brown with darker marks. The incubation period is nineteen to twenty-eight days. The babies are feathered upon hatching and can generally feed themselves. They leave the nest in thirty to sixty-five days. There is one brood or set of eggs per year.

Fun Fact: In 1848, Utah was infested with locusts. They were killing the crops and threatening the residents with famine. Seagulls flew in from the lake islands and ate all the locusts and saved the crops and the people. To show their gratitude, the people of Utah declared the "seagull" as their state bird.

MULLET

\'mə-lət\

Classification
Kingdom: Animalia (Animals)
Phylum: Chordata (Vertabrates)
Class: Actinopterygii (Ray-finned)
Order: Mugiliformes (Mullet fish)
Family: Mugilidae (Mullet)

Description: The typical mullet will grow to about a foot and a half in length and weigh only about two pounds. They generally take on a very light color scheme and are scaled across their bodies from the base of their fins to their tails. They are typically green or bluish green on top, have a light silver hue on the sides and are white underneath. Their faces are somewhat beak-like and they have small noses and mouths. The distinguishing characteristic on these fish is their large bellies that are significantly rounded and muscular underneath.

Habitat: Mullet are typically found naturally in the southern Atlantic and Gulf regions of the United States and all around the coast of South America. They can also be found in and around Australia and Indonesia, as well as around the eastern parts of Africa.

Food: Mullet commonly grub about in the sand or mud for microscopic plants, small animals, and other food.

Life Cycle: Once a year, the female lays around 6,000 to 16,000 eggs that are very small and these eggs incubate for three to seven days before becoming larvae. After four to six days, the larvae become tiny fish that are about one-half to one inch long.

Fun Fact: Mullet are often bred on fish farms for food for other fish.

SEA OAT

\'sē 'ōt\

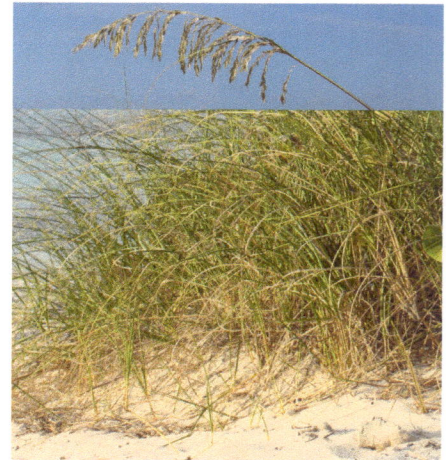

Classification
Kingdom: Plantae (Plants)
Group: Monocots (One seed leaves)
Order: Poales (Grasses, bromeliads, sedges)
Family: Poaceae (Grasses)
Genus: Uniola (Perennial grasses)
Species: Paniculata (Sea oat)

Description: Sea oats are usually the most visible plant growing on the sand dunes behind wave-washed beaches. It grows from underground stems (called rhizomes) in long colonies where the winds shift and swirl the sand. The leaves are up to two feet long and one inch wide. In summertime, the six-foot aboveground stems (called culms) end in gracefully drooping eighteen-inch clusters (called panicles) of flat, yellowish and one and one-half inch long seed heads called spikelets.

Location: Sea oats grow on sand dunes along the Atlantic coast from Virginia to Florida and around the Gulf to eastern Mexico and in the northern West Indies (Caribbean Islands).

Features: Able to put up with salt, sea oats are often used in sand dune stabilization programs because its extensive system of underground stems and roots helps reduce erosion. The dried and cooked seeds are said to make a flavorful cereal. The mature seedheads are very decorative and commonly used in dried flower arrangements.

WARNING: Wild sea oats are protected in Florida and Georgia (and probably other states as well), not because it is endangered or threatened, but because it performs a valuable ecological service by stabilizing sand dunes. It is illegal to pick wild sea oats.

SEA GRAPE

\'sē 'grāp\

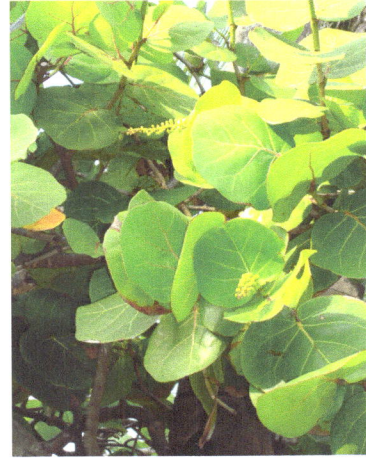

Classification
Kingdom: Plantae (Plants)
Group: Magnoliopsida (Two seed leaves)
Order: Caryophyllales (Flowering, fleshy stems, leaves)
Family: Polygonacae (Knotweed, many knees)
Genus: Coccoloba (Evergreen, alternate leaves)
Species: Uvifera (Sea grape)

Description: On sand dunes and beaches, sea grape usually grows as a sprawling shrub with solid branches and rarely a clear trunk. However, away from the constant salt and sand spray it can grow into a handsome vase-shaped tree up to 50 feet tall. The shiny, evergreen leaves are leathery, rounded with heart-shaped bases. The bright green leaves are often veined in red and are about eight inches in diameter. The fragrant white flowers are very small and found on six to ten inch spikes. Female trees bare reddish fruits that are about three-quarters inch in diameter, pear-shaped and fleshy with a hard "stone." They hang down in grape-like clusters and attract birds and children.

Location: Sea grape is a tropical plant, native to coastal hammocks, coastal scrub, coastal grasslands and beach strands from Argentina north throughout the West Indies and the Florida Keys to Pinellas County on the Gulf Coast and southern Volusia County on the Atlantic Coast of Florida. It does not reach tree heights at the northern limits of its range.

Features: The fruits are edible raw and are made into "seaside jelly" or wine. In the West Indies, they boil the wood to yield a red dye. Wood from larger trees is used for cabinet work. A gum from the bark is used for throat ailments and the roots are used to treat dysentery.

MORNING GLORY

\'mor-niŋ 'glor-ē\

Classification
Kingdom: Plantae (Plants)
Group: Asterids (Flowering plants)
Order: Solanales (Nightshade)
Family: Convolvulaceae (Bindweeds)
Genus: Ipomoea (Twining, trailing)
Species: Pescaprae (Morning glory)

Description: Morning glory or "Beach Morning Glory" can cover hundred feet lengths as it races along the beach, but it never gets more than a few inches high. This is an evergreen perennial (flowers every year) with a large, thick root that can be ten feet long and two inches in diameter. The stem is flexible, one-half inch in diameter, branches freely and roots at the nodes (where the leafs meet the stems). The fleshy leathery leaves are about four inches long and carried on stalks that are six inches long. The leaves looked kind of like the imprint of a goat's foot that gives the plant its nickname of "Goat's Foot." The flowers are pink to lavender purple and are about two inches long. Each flower opens only once, in the morning, but new ones keep coming almost all year long, peaking from May through November.

Location: Morning glory grows on sand dunes and beaches above the high tide line in tropical and subtropical regions throughout the world. In the U.S., it occurs on the coast from Texas to Florida to Georgia. Morning glory is a pioneer plant, often associated with sea oats, defending the beach against erosion.

Features: There are about 500 species of morning glories. Some, like cypress vine and moonflower, are pretty ornamentals. One version, sweet potato, is an important and delicious food crop. The name, "Beach Morning Glory," usually refers to a species with white flowers that also grows on the beach.

Social and Academic Lessons

Moral to the Story:

Be happy with who you are. Everyone has a special gift.
– Celebrate your gifts.

"Modern Discipline" Principles:

Confident Voice: Stand up tall, look the person in the eye and tell them assertively what you did not like and what you want them to do the next time instead.

It is important for children to stand up for themselves and increase self-esteem. Teaching a child to use their confident voice, guiding a child to use it and then watching a child use it independently is critical for a child to protect themselves and reduce bullying.

First, if a child seems upset about something that has happened, describe to the child what you see. For example, "Your face looks like this (and make your face upset like their face), and your hands are like this (make your hands into fists if that is what they are doing). Something must have happened." The child may say, "Johnny pushed me to get into line first."

You would then say, "Did you like it?" If the child says, "Yes" then you may say, "Well, if you ever don't like it, you can use your confident voice to tell them to stop." If they say, "No" then you may say, "Well, if you don't like it, I can help you use your confident voice. Stand up straight and look Johnny in the eye and say using your confident voice, "I don't like it when you push me. Get in line at the end." Have the child practice it with you first and have the child repeat the words to you. If the child says it either too soft or really aggressive, then say, "Match your voice to mine and say it again assertively." Have the child practice until the child is using their confident voice assertively without being overly aggressive or too soft. Then tell the child that you are both going over to Johnny and are going to do the same thing. Walk over and have the child use their confident voice to deliver the message. Look at Johnny for an appropriate response - which is either "ok" or "I am sorry" or "I will get to the end of the line." Facilitate Johnny going to the end of the line. It is important that afterward you celebrate with the child with comments such as "You did it! You used your confident voice to tell him what you wanted. Good for you."

Other confident voice examples:

Susan grabs the toy from Karen – "I don't like it when you grab my toy. Instead ask, "When you are done, may I have a turn please?""

Robert calls Mathew a name – "I don't like it when you call me names. Use my name "Mathew" when you want my attention."

Stacey burps loud in Martha's face – "I don't like it when you burp in my face. If you have to burp, use a napkin or go to the restroom."

Stephen laughs at Richard – "I don't like it when you laugh at me. Please stop."

Listening to others: Have a discussion with the child about the importance of listening to others. Talk about how some of the lizards stopped laughing when Larry used his confident voice but how some did not. Brainstorm ideas to do when others don't listen (examples: ask for help, take a breath and walk away or laugh it off).

Celebrating: It is important for children to celebrate. Talk about how Larry did the happy lizard dance to celebrate. The "Happy Lizard Dance" goes like this – Two hops forward, two hops backwards, a hop to the left and a hop to the right. Do a lizard run in place, put one fist up and then pull down your arm and fist to your side with a emphatic "YES!" You can also do this fun lizard dance to any music.

Deep Breathing: It is important to deep breathe to help the brain function properly. Have the child practice breathing in through their nose and out through their mouth with a longer exhale than inhale. When the child breathes in, their stomach should go out and expand. When the child exhales, their stomach should deflate. Don't have the child breathe big, fast breaths that make their shoulders go up. Instead, have the child concentrate on their slow breathing and focus on the correct breathing technique. This will optimize their brain's capabilities.

Feelings: Have the child change their "I am sad" or "I am mad" statements to "I feel sad" or "I feel mad." The child's whole being is not sad or mad – it is just their feelings at the time. Don't let the feeling consume the child. Make sure the child feels the feeling, keeps breathing and assures themselves that they can handle anything.

LANGUAGE ARTS/WRITING

Book Report: Have the child create a book report about the story or have them do a combination of a one-page book report and a "hands on" activity such as a poster, puppets, diorama box, claymation or paper mache lizard or dragonfly. This can be coordinated with art lessons.

Onomatopoeia: Find the sound words with the child in the story. Talk about how they help bring the story to life. "Buzzzz" and "Whoosh" are some examples in the story. Create your own onomatopoeia with the child for this story or for your own story.

Punctuation: Talk about how the punctuation helps us to understand the story. Discuss how and why the periods, commas, quotations, question marks, exclamation marks are used. Find examples in the story. Put example sentences from the story on a chalkboard or piece of paper without punctuation and then have the child add the correct punctuation.

"Said" is Overused: Brainstorm other ways to show conversation besides always using "said." The examples in the book include: asked, queried, proclaimed, stated, replied, responded, exclaimed, explained, answered, continued, shouted, whispered and Daryl told Larry.

MATH

Problem Solving: Create and solve problems using characters and experiences from the story. Have the child create a number sentence for each problem and to show their work used to arrive at the answer. For example:

Addition – There were 4 lizards playing in the sea oats. 6 more joined in the fun. How many lizards in all were playing? Answer: The number sentence is 4 plus 6 equals 10 and the complete sentence answer would be: There were 10 lizards in all playing in the sea oats.

Subtraction – 9 lizards were laughing at Larry. Larry used his confident voice and told them to stop. 7 lizards stop laughing. How many lizards were still laughing at Larry? Answer: The number sentence is 9 minus 7 equals 2 and the complete sentence answer would be: There were 2 lizards still laughing at Larry.

Multiplication – The dragonflies flew in groups when they played tag. There were 5 groups of 3 dragonflies playing. What was the total number of dragonflies playing tag? Answer: The number sentence is 5 times 3 equals 15 and the complete sentence answer would be: There were 15 dragonflies in total playing tag.

Division – There were 20 lizards. They got in groups of 5 to celebrate Larry's flying. How many groups of lizards were there to celebrate with Larry? Answer: The number sentence would be 20 divided by 5 equals 4 and the complete sentence answer would be: There were 4 groups of lizards celebrating with Larry.

SCIENCE

Reports: Assign a science topic found in the book to individuals or a group and have them generate a report. Teach utilizing the appendices. The topics may include: anole lizard, dragonfly, seagull, sea oat, sea grape, mullet and morning glory.

Field Trip: Visit a beach or a science center and look at the various plants and animals that are there. You can discuss the various things you see. Discuss how the things you see are the same or different from the plants and animals in the story.

ART

Drawing: Have the children draw a picture of their favorite character in a new adventure or scene from their own experience at a beach.

Collage: Collect seashells, fallen leaves, sand or other items from the beach and glue them on construction paper to create your own beach scene.

MUSIC

Singing: Have the children sign along (to the tune of "Mary Had a Little Lamb") and play instruments or clap.

Larry was a small lizard, small lizard, small lizard.
Larry was a small lizard, who could not fly at all.

Larry made a friend one day, friend one day, friend one day.
Larry made a friend one day, this friend was named Daryl.

Daryl was a dragonfly, dragonfly, dragonfly.
Daryl was a dragonfly with wings that flapped real fast.

Daryl helped him fly real high, fly real high, fly real high.
Daryl helped him fly real high and Larry felt real good.

Creating Music: See if you can create your own song to go along with the story by changing words from a favorite song or create a new song altogether.

GLOSSARY

Accomplishment – achieving of something
Adventure – exciting experience
Amazement – astonishment; surprise; wonder
Assertively – acting confidently, strong and pronounced
Astonishment – great amazement; surprise; wonder
Camouflage – concealment; disguise
Celebrated – show happiness at something, praise something
Concerned – anxious or worried, interested, involved
Courage – quality of being brave
Exclaimed – talked loudly and suddenly
Explained – describe; clarify
Horizon – place where earth meets the sky
Majestic – impressive
Overcome – conquer problem, win despite obstacles
Particular – one out of several
Politely – well-mannered
Proclaimed – declare something publicly
Queried – to ask a question
Realized – know and understand something
Reminded – cause to think of something
Shallow – not deep
Soar – fly, glide high
Swirled – turn with circular motion, spiral
Swooped – making a sweeping decent, pounce
Thud – dull heavy sound

About the Author and Illustrator

About the author Kim Whitney:

Kim Whitney has a Bachelors Degree in Elementary Education and a Masters Degree in Educational Leadership. She has extensive experience in progressive education including being a teacher in elementary education for six years, a learning specialist in a middle school for two years, an assistant principal in elementary education for two years and a principal at an elementary school for eight years. Kim has attended multiple seminars on discipline as well as brain research over the years and has been a guest speaker at educational seminars on the subjects. Kim loves traveling and is enjoying the motherhood adventure. She has combined her love of reading books and going to the beach in authoring this book.

About the illustrator Deborah Allison:

Deborah Allison has studied art in America and abroad. She has a Bachelors of Fine Art Degree in Painting and Graphic Design and a Masters Degree of Art in Design Illustration. For many years, she worked as an art director and designer, but now enjoys painting commissioned artwork and murals. Deborah is inspired by the beauty and energy of nature. Striking colors and unique perspectives are signatures of her work. As a mother of two boys, Deborah believes in the power of great books and vivid illustrations to develop young minds. To view more art by Deborah Allison go to: www.deborahallisonart.com

www.ingramcontent.com/pod-product-compliance
Lightning Source LLC
Chambersburg PA
CBHW060813090426

42737CB00002B/54